GEOGRAPHIES OF SOUL AND TAFFETA

Sarah Sarai

Also by Sarah Sarai
The Future Is Happy
Emily Dickinson's Coconut Face
Oh You of the Cotton Pajamas!
The Risen Barbie
I Feel Good

GEOGRAPHIES OF SOUL AND TAFFETA

Sarah Sarai

© 2016 Sarah Sarai

Book design: kd diamond
Cover art: Justin Alves

Published by Indolent Books,
an imprint of Indolent Enterprises, LLC

www.indolentbooks.com
Brooklyn, New York

ISBN: 978-1-945023-04-0

CONTENTS

An Interrogatory...7

Anyway...8

Miracle Fiber..9

The Crew Is Restless and I Am Sick at Heart...............................10

(Marc Jacobs to the West Village.)..11

I was much too far out all my life. 12

Angels Talk to Me at Bus Stops...13

White Tunnel and the Night Return..14

Fabian Averanius (Arthur Craven)...16

As She Crosses...17

Rolling on the Floor Killing Elves...18

We Knew How...20

Popular Mechanics..21

Legend With Usual Cruelties...22

Family...23

The Princess Memoir..24

Love Letter...26

But Then Again...27

Commerce for the Good of the Peoples.......................................29

Andy Warhol Left Those Parties by Midnight............................31

It Is True and Truth Sometimes Gets Me Published..................33

On the Way to the Gallery...35

The End. 36

Popularity..38

Stop...39

Someone Is Knocking at My Door...40

An Interrogatory

> Nothing but smooth sailing.
> —*The Isley Brothers*

Those aren't birds are they are they,
are they?, or are they insects of an ilk

glowing and hovering hummingbird-
like though not hummingbird, not bird,

no, I see it, that which I wasn't seeing,
a lingering phosphorescence, no

luminescence, oh!, it is incandescence
and those are seraphim I see, I am

seeing seraphim, six-winged seraphim,
seraphim having six wings or so said

Isaiah, a seraphim seer, two wings, fans
over a mighty face, two enfolding feet

and two neon wings to lift them aloft,
smoothly sail above prophesies for our

tangled times, two wings golden as honey
is gold, as amber is gold, as transparency

is gold, carry us to a feared eternal now,
tolerable, almost, when we sing along.

Anyway

I was so happy when Mickey Rooney
showed up in *The Black Stallion*, 1978.
It had been awhile and there he was
with his hello, folks! face gone serious,
still warm and visually, believably wise.
Clarence Muse drove a horse and wagon.
Pauline Kael, the film critic, wrote that
being black, Clarence Muse was
a spiritual stereotype, a limiting code.
I get it but I liked seeing him, anyway.
Muse was born in 1899. In 1976
he played "Snapper" in *Car Wash*.
This poem is now over because soon
as I write "Car Wash," the portable
stereo that is my brain sings "Workin'
at the car wash, yeah" and that's that.
Just as well. Thoughts of Ms. Kael
bring to mind that atrocity *Noah* which
situates Mount Ararat in Middle Earth
where everyone's white and crusty.
Trust me or I'll have to quote Kael
who called Russell Crowe a slab
of a man (*Gladiator* 2002) and God
frowns on bad-mouthing. The End.

Miracle Fiber

It's the weirdest thing,
to be in love with a woman.
Nothing else matters.
Even that campy hate scorn is
rickrack on a little black dress—
you kidding me?

Your woman is a body of miracle fiber,
a tote accommodating
a change of clothes and good shampoo,
a heated embrace, an epicenter,
a little sun next to you
preparing you for your dangerous salvation.

You have to find a way
and a Sherpa anxious to
    shake out, lean over,
    anchor raw minerals
on the four directions,
the four elements,
the nonrefundable missteps.

God is whatever makes us better.
Who's seen Her, besides
    William Blake
    and ten million mothers.
Do they agree how shining her hair is
or that her voice is the unified theory
of everything arranged for strings?

The idea is to be led to something
that is not you.
If it is the solar system in your arms,
pinging you, well, that works.

The Crew Is Restless and I Am Sick at Heart

Had to form my own resistance movement.
Had to write, *I have good feelings*
about the journey but fear battles with myself.
Had to work black felt to a beret.
Had to suck cinders into swampy bellow.
Had to buy Erik Little Cigars
from an Amish farmer.
Had to be surprised.
Had to find them on Twenty-Third and Third.
Had to quit.
Had to just had to envision BBC kings
fighting brother France
on green-island fields,
hear hoofbeats of scythed Mongols
thunder on the steppes.
Had to smile because there is a field
in battlefield.
But of course there is also a battle.

(Marc Jacobs to the West Village.)

A stop before a sign is one way to go.
When time is up, you'll be history.
Name your poison, said the barkeep.
Fear and trembling, I responded. *And Netflix.*
A priest, a rabbi and a minister walk into a wall.
Who, if I cried out, would hear me on
the escalator to the 7 train?
The grenade launch went quite well,
don't you think?
Sweetheart, one day all this will be tours.
(Marc Jacobs to the West Village.)
When Trouble farts, you can smell it.
If your number's up, you're not in Australia.
Sleep tight, dearest drunk.
Officer, arrest that Spam! Hope he fries.
Your cautious hit man uses a Bunsen burner.
What did the linoleum square say?
One day all this will be floors.
One day? All this will be floors.

I was much too far out all my life.

after Stevie Smith

And not waving but drowning
And not wading but drowning
Not parading but drowning
And not treading but drowning
And not slogging but weighted
Not waiting but over my head
In a suck of the ocean a war
With the turf of the lost and the
Bloated leagues buried down
Not wallowing but downing
A cocktail of bitters of seaweed
Too much for the lubbers not
Winking not waving but lapping
The last of a life far offshore.

Angels Talk to Me at Bus Stops

> I have had very peculiar and strange experiences.
> —*Minnesota Multiple Personality Index*

And if they're not messengers
flimsy at bus stops
their looping carousel ting
in dozing ears.

And if they're not messengers
jolting sleep at 2 a.m.
pfp fpf fpf pfp
oh starry commotion.

And if they're not messengers
a third heartbeat thrumming
thunder-dark room
minimally the medium.

And if not, then presentation,
installation on space
time and the fleeting.
Everything can be ransacked.

Predestination is a process offered
the body by the stars.

And if a messenger then
a thistle buzzing summer air,
and if not that, a lie.

White Tunnel and the Night Return

I was vessel, dumb animal receptor.
DNA snaked me into life,
three insurrectionist rivers carried me.
Antiquity was my patron saint.

I heard a call before I heard a call,
an off-rhythm more fluid than any
legacy code patriarchal in my cells.
A woman floating, I splashed
oceanic palms my sisters envied,
light-years off. I have been lucky.

Jesus, dance with me.
Mary, in your arms.

No one said anything, let alone,
It will be easy.
The writers said, It will be hard,
ethics and a capacity for reason and doubt,
a daily crucifixion.
The shills asked for Barabbas.
Every freakin' day. Barabbas!

Jesus, dance with me.
Mary, in your arms.

Just now I prayed the Kindness
funnel herself to this subway car.
I am wet clay, not the wind.
I can't part seas of red, infirmity
from body, rage from the raging.

Dance with me, Jesus.
Hold me, Mary.

You must have the strength of
Ozymandias and consider his stupidity,

a "heart that feeds"—a "hand that mocks."

There is nothing out of place, Jesus.
Hold me, Mary. I might be wrong.

Fabian Avenarius (Arthur Craven)

> I can be anything. Leave me in the dark.
> —*Jorge Francisco Isidoro Luis Borges*

I was christened Contessa Lucinda Mujer de la Dia de Muertos.
Crones called me often,
my nurse called me Sibyl,
the workers, spoiled and worth it.

The world was my lover, the oyster my best friend.
Women called me wanton,
my husband, cock, tease, rapture,
my wife in the bleak of the night, "So beautiful."

On my bed of many feathers, wings, many wings
dreaming five fields of chrysanthemums.
Rose-red. Cumulous. Sunrise. Amontillado.
And Flesh, a sixth field of Flesh.

"So beautiful, so very beautiful."

As She Crosses

A street wide as that leather belt
she wished she didn't own—it's
not her she's not a leather belt
crossing and sensing an elephant-
trunk foreign on her calves causing
her a start for it's a danger to cross
anyone and yes we took a vote to
that French café on Seventh for
a night out as we couldn't take it
for a night in at least not in a way
you could wrap your head around
if your head were Turkish as a
towel as she crosses the street
which could be a lane though
she sees a trunk of steam toddling
after a screamer trunk a shriek
of fasteners murmur of paper clips
murder of scratch pads brace of
staples flock of Bics clattering
of pushpins a creamer coalition
and a lullaby of Broadway which
will be crossed but what puzzles
as she sets a foot, most likely her
own, off the curb is a taxi nudging
ornaments of someone's girlhood
her unpacked friends consider
common is she has wings and
lifts off when thunderous joy of
sorrow as felt by two elephants
reunited after years of cruelty and
separation, search for the YouTubes,
crosses its loopy shadow on her
path about which we'd expostulate
but look there, she is so happy so
very happy, with her head in the
clouds and her feet nearly nearby.

Rolling on the Floor Killing Elves

The elves, the freaking elves.
They laugh at huge clumsy humans.
Big hands, big feet, and have you seen
our big bent stinky shoes!

Elves gather 'round our big bent
stinky shoes and toast with their grimy
elf tankards of dew gone rank and
dreams we just can't remember.
They clutch their sharp elf sides,
slap each other with gnarled elf hands.

We are glad *someone*
is having a good time.

We want to, damn it, remember last
night's dream with a road *and* a house,
with a road and a house *and* our sister,
who died. We never dream about her
though she's checked in on us once
or twice, same as our mother and father.

Our father says,
That El Greco knew how to paint!

Our mother was a woman with
a tough life, but also daughters,
four intelligent originals she loved.
One of whom, our undreamed sister,
is the only of us up there, so far.
She tinkered in our dream, that
house, that road. And then?

Stop laughing at us, elves!
(They don't.)

Maybe that's what my sister is telling me.
Roll on the floor, kid, kill the elves.
Kill every last one of them.

We Knew How

We waited for our laptops to recognize our sovereignty.
        Were comforted by a lavender mist on our desktops.
We reflected on "Desktop."
        Trying to be retrospectively insightful we remembered
Our teens. We stained our desk maple.
        Might not have been maple.
We were okay with that.
        Caffeine deep-muscled our nerves though nerves
Are not what you'd call *muscular*.
        We noticed our walk-to-work shoes were silver.
Our at-work shoes slept in their file drawer.
        Slatterns. We wondered about coworkers'
Bank accounts and sex lives.
        We resisted the call of the cat video.
Checked *The Guardian* online.
        No news is good news.
Work came our way. Editing and annotation.
        Late afternoon was slower than the five turtles on Sunday.
They posed as Nobility for a sculptor we made up.
        We hoped god was having a good day.
And that she'd push us to go out and find a woman.
        We suggested a few billion lives be made easier.
Her attention was diverted.
        She liked to juggle stars to amuse the god
A galaxy over. We closed our programs and
        Clicked Shut Down. We suspected lady god
Wanted to do that. To force the machine off.
        Be all about juggling. We gave her a thumbs-up,
Hoping to gain her approval.
        We reconciled ourselves to being unnoticed.
Decided it didn't matter.
        We knew how to turn on our computer.

Popular Mechanics

By way of electron molecule
scattering, rotational excitation,
ball bearings greased up and
scooting down pinball chutes,
the body confirms its presence
in our lives. It's psychedelic.
Personal history, the day-to-day,
is a quick-shuffle card trick.
Perspective is another illusion,
riches being indistinguishable
from chambers of pathos.
But let's return to the moment
we walk out the door to get
the mail which may arrive or not,
keeping us giddy in trepidation
of the surprise of corners.
Friend, I know it's not easy.
That's the point. Look at me,
a poet of many sorrows.
Yet I summon my house keys
and inner child and somehow,
lowliest I, rank of moral fiber
but game, act *as if* I were charmed.
And behold I *am* ignited *and*
awake to hear the preacher's
rhapsodic subway lament:
we are low and need charging,
and someone is hungry, *hungry,*
half a sandwich could help.

Legend With Usual Cruelties

A thousand-year redwood—
one ring encircling the other—
concentrically outdoing in circumference—
protecting—what grew before.
Dimensions beyond the obvious are
science, fiction, legend an adolescent will wrap her
mind around concentrically—
that there could be
replicas of her, unaware of her or wrapping
a parallel mind around a possibility of replication.
So legend replicates legend. Thus,
you are legend despite merely requisite
dimensions and flyaway hair with its layers
of disobedience and gleam.
You are a legend with usual cruelties.
You are a legend because one day you are kind
and don't laugh at the poet saying
struggle could end if only.
You're a legend because you picked up a leaf,
a red leaf, and tried to figure, its spine now brittle like
your grandmother and thin but beautiful
how it grew on that tree and after a season
of impudent green, turned color,
like the sky will, every night, and
fluttered to brown hard earth.
They are talking of you even
now in a dimension transecting folly,
of your queasy appreciation of the gift.
So, beloved, you can sleep, and rest,
assured you inspire in more than one world.

Family

My three siblings are older than I am.
The biggest Russian doll who
contains we younger is Jean,
and it is with her I saw the movie *Jaws*.

For *The Exorcist* I just went along with
a loose assemblage, friends of friends.
That's what you do with movies,
you see them, even if it's the first
day and you are blithe as a donut on
an oblong tray at Winchell's.
If the Vatican set up a table in
the theater lobby like Seventh Day
Adventists in the subways I'd have
signed up for a catechism class on
the spot. That was some scary shit.

One time Jean sent me a clipping from
the *San Francisco Examiner*.
Two sisters, 76 and 82ish, lived together
on Nob Hill until the older murdered
the younger. *Watch your back, kid,*
Jean printed in the margin.

I knew *Jaws* was going to be epic,
am unsurprised by this future of
plastic predators-of-the-seas rising from
bubble baths on *Saturday Night Live*.
But when the shark leapt from an
endless ocean of lost whalers, Jean
and me, we screamed, we shrieked,
we grabbed each other's hands.

Before and after *Jaws* I have known terror.
That was the only time I ever held my sister's hand.

The Princess Memoir

Once I slept on a fork.
There was no other way to convince me
I am no princess.

Curse originality in isolation.

Doors of perception squeak.
Someone knows when you're
busting through.

There's no breaching Heaven
on a feather-Babel,
no up escalator, no
stairway curled as an old hippie's
fingernail.

What is is and
the goose ameliorates nothing.

In Hell there is a waterslide to
Satan's cold butt.
Why freeze, friend,
when just a gesture would undue?

And why did the translator hate you
when you said you'd read King James?

You've seen eternity in the airspace.
It will not always be 2:41 a.m.
The station on 14th will recharge.
38th to downtown will glitter.

There was a time you scoffed at
the three-inch mattress pad
which even now will not deliver you.

But when you are blinded in the streets
lifts you to a sort of sleep.
With odds for and against waking.

Love Letter

The EpiPens I gave you.
The medical marijuana you
smuggled from New Jersey.
The time you rushed in
with a job lead on your phone.
I got the damn job.
It was twenty percent creative.
Which they'd promised.
Which made you excited for me.
Excited? I thought you loved me.
Planks are laid over my volcano.
No splinters, not a one.
You had me rub the Greek stone
before I walked over.
The old ways working, working well.
I would have climbed into you.
Every woman has her limits?
Like I don't know that.
Like that doesn't tear me apart.

But Then Again

That's how it works.
You're stuck in a dream
and without knowing
much of anything make
the best of it and if not
the best, an absolute mess,
causing your airy head
to like a stone sink into
your cold-sweat palms,
elbows strafing an endless
desk of industrial and
post-industrial horror—
the modern world.
You suspect God's an
anarchist and admit you
like belief which transforms
you into an archangel, a
nimbus, the celebrating
Sun. Who knows what
anything means and all
that given all that may be
a load of crap and so may
anything unless there is
no load. Unless this phase
is waltzing us—*one* two
three—*one* two three—
through a dust-mote galaxy
where someone, say,
Spinoza, sips cocoa or
Yemenite coffee grown in
Amsterdam's botanical
gardens. Through lenses
ground to a halt sees life as
a run-through, considers
a compassionate mover's
blueprints for lives of virtue
or indolence subcontracted

to each of us at birth, sees
artists sipping coffee and
revelation. Sees his sister,
Spinoza's sister, why not,
Mozart had one. Emotionally
curious like he is she sights
a presence surpassing logic,
like he does, something in
our universe surpassing pain.

Commerce for the Good of the Peoples

At the shop of good moral character you
bought five grams of valor and
a strong chin

For your love, essence of steadfast heart
in a vial

Good gosh, that's pricey stuff

You speculated over glasses
Horn of Africa-rimmed so you could
spot a swarthy pirate, yo-ho

For your love you thought, Titanium frames!
because

You passed on the steady gaze for its claim on
concentration
There's only so much
good moral character a person can stand
in a day

You and your love pledged to
utilize purchases
soon as you were home and
would have but for a stop
for wines and tidbits,
brandy and later a few tokes
from that joint
in the car ashtray

Anyway
your love left her steadfast heart
in the Audi whilst the cat ate
your strong chin (at least *you*
brought your purchase into the house)

You and your love split the valor
Everything's better with two forks and whipped cream

Andy Warhol Left Those Parties by Midnight

> Sorrow everywhere.
> —Jack Gilbert

You will not wake at 7
tomorrow morning and
start working as I've read
he did, will not wonder until
9 or 11 a.m. if you can fly
Berthe to San Francisco
to confirm sorrow everywhere.

You created Berthe in a story.
She is a character,
and if you exit the club
with only that lilac tattoo
on the kissable dip of
your wrist you will work
on her in the morning
like she is a face and you are
plastic surgeon to the stars
instead of a writer of stories
you are not sure anyone reads.
There is a woman.

Her breath is jasmine, no,
hibiscus, no, ancient—
an Egyptian myrrh
rubbed on the royal dead
who foresaw death as
beloved of symbolists
who see you in thresholds
and on a journey.

Beneath a silver globe
of disco you and the real woman
are felines howling.
Her dress of velvet mauve.

Oil-of-lavender skin.
A baby-breath nipple caressed
by a crushed strap sliding.

Andy Warhol would
slip away to a life of control
and productivity,
two words at a loss on
a dance floor with a remote
of secret flesh, in mirrors.

It Is True and Truth Sometimes Gets Me Published

My sisters and I are lost each according to her merits.
I will be killed if I say more.

Consider me, the youngest.
A natural-born floater downy with plumage

I've followed three quacks o'er the fishy seas.
In our heads are captains' charts of

crackling parchment and family secrets.
Nothing is invincible. Not everything's a clue.

It isn't the culture or wide-armed greeting
of the new shebang we skip.

Instructions are a hard swallow.
Anyway, someone booked me passage

on this ship of four fools sailing
into a storm meteorologists have named

Colossal Congenital Disappointment.
Or did I sign on for this?

That's a very good question, yes, thank you.
Expectations should be lowered, like

a visor when steering into the sun.
Is it time to be chipper?

What does time mean to a vessel on an egg
used by Christopher Columbus as object lesson?

The unexamined life is worth living.
Before any conference or new endeavor

read all documentation.
It doesn't take brains, this thing called happiness,

often confused with success and a great sex life.
Easy enough to be confused.

On the Way to the Gallery

Never allow Greeks near your conjuring.
The cult of primordial Nyx,

aboriginal goddess of chiffon,
foremother to tricked and tricking

Hera   Aphrodite   Athena—that crew
—hissed at my augur of

feline elemental mists
geographies of soul and taffeta.

On the way to the gallery I conjured
(cut grass   the levitating sun)

(a tangerine id peeled for juice and pulp
by a woman's ten pads and rubbed

by her heavy books of life)—I conjured
satin   a personal trainer   faint morning stars.

Goddesses wreak easy havoc with enchantment,
a garment flattering to only a few.

The End.

Leaving Michelangelo
you were smitten—
hear how the word
stops you without the
exit sign of a line break?
smitten—
by Joos van Cleve's
Last Judgment—
hordes straining to see
Jesus-on-a-chair like
a bridegroom hoisted.

Your high school
English teacher said
Billy Budd was
a Christ stand-in.
Melville wrote the novella
on the site of the old
Lexington Avenue Armory.
Your high school principal
said only gays wore
polka-dot neckties.
He was quite a theorist.

That hyphen in *Moby-Dick*,
written by Melville in
Massachusetts, is really
a harpoon aimed at
profiteers' hearts.
Home from Iraq,
women and men in fatigues
catch a smoke on
the monster's concrete steps.
A cathedral-sky is
no ceiling on the lies.

Jesus rides oblivious to
miseries of poor judgment
while Michelangelo looks
snappy in a polka-dot tie.
Your high school principal
wants to apologize.

Popularity

Snakes are pretty damn famous.
More than they deserve to be.
I've slithered on the sand.
Snapped my fangs at an ankle.
Soaked sun, rock-snoozed.
I dig the desert.
Have I told you that?
How much I dig the desert?
Low desert, high desert, any desert.
Name a desert. Sahara?
Dig it. Name another one.
Gobi? Good choice! Mojave?
Been there, done it, hankering to do it again.
Also, I'm a very spiritual person.
Another life I was a prophet.
Prophets. Deserts. Hello?
How spiritual is a snake?
Can a snake hiss like an angel?
I can. Hisssssssssssss.
Hey, fuck you for doubting me.
I should be more famous than a stupid snake.

Stop

In an ad agency, Traffic is like
Department of the Shepherds,
or an escort service,
housemother, Charon,
ferrying files from account exec. to writer
to art director to the shop to editorial
back to writer, exec., client, hell.
When the agency is pharm, the ad
could be direct-to-physician, direct-to-
patient, include an ISI (Important Safety Information).
Pharm. pays better than general advertising but each
ad has me fighting early training:
this is a load of crap.
Remember, I wasn't allowed medicine as a kid.
When I was headed to Camp Yallani we needed
a doc to sign off.
He spotted weeping sores on my hand.
What's that? he asked Mom.
It's nothing she said.
Don't blame advertisers for the public's foolishness.
David Ogilvy's *Little Red Book*
of selling-relevant aphorisms
had typos.
Mao's *Little Red Book* fell to
reform and reeducation through labor.
There's no poetry in consumerism or
totalitarianism.
Oh save us from our leaders.
All of us.

Someone Is Knocking at My Door

I spill oatmeal on my new blouse.
I dab dish soap and water over the oatmeal on my new blouse,
then shreds of paper toweling over the dish soap and
water on the oatmeal I spilled on my new blouse.
What message am I trying to send and why didn't I send it
      by email?
Someone is knocking at my door.

No one buzzed so I figure, Jehovah's Witnesses, known to
      drift past lobby keyholes in their sensible dress,
armed with pamphlets like muskets to home Sunday-school us.
Are they hoping to save me from annihilation and
can I persuade them I'm okay with annihilation?
Someone is knocking at my door.

I look to the peephole. Tolstoy Augustine Virgil Flaubert.
"Why have your affections waned? Are you a man hater?"
      Hater! Hater! echoes in the hall.
Leibniz adjusts his wig.
Save the dead! Long live the dead! the petition on
their clipboards reads.
Someone is knocking at my door.

ACKNOWLEDGMENTS

These poems appeared, sometimes in different versions, in the following publications.

Ascent: "But Then Again"
The Collagist: "I was much too far out all my life."
Cordite Poetry Journal: "Fabian Avenarius (Arthur Craven)"
decomP magazinE: "We Knew How"
Lyre Lyre: "The Crew Is Restless and I Am Sick at Heart"
Other Rooms Press: "As She Crosses," "(Marc Jacobs to the West Village)"
Ping-Pong: "Miracle Fiber"
Painted Bride Quarterly: "Anyway," and "Popularity"
Pool Poetry: "Commerce for the Good of the Peoples," "On the Way to the Gallery"
Posit: "It Is True and Truth Sometimes Gets Me Published," "Popular Mechanics," "White Tunnel and the Night Return"
The Writing Disorder: "Andy Warhol Left Those Parties by Midnight,"

"I was much too far out all my life." is a tribute to Stevie Smith (1902–1971) and her often cited poem "Not Waving but Drowning."

My gratitude to Debora Lidov who with genius and patience read this collection and offered invaluable comments; Christine Hamm for her generous insight and for ladies lunching; Joanna Fuhrman who has a bounty of prompts and suggested the title; r. erica doyle who gave me courage; the splendid design crew at Indolent Books; and to Michael Broder, whose tenacity and kindness inspire.

ABOUT THE AUTHOR

Sarah Sarai was born in Port Washington, grew up in California, and now lives in New York. She is a former English teacher and college professor and is now an editor and researcher. She has an MFA in fiction from Sarah Lawrence College. Books/chapbooks include *The Future Is Happy* (Blaze VOX [Books]); *I Feel Good, Emily Dickinson's Coconut Face*, and *The Risen Barbie*. Her poems appear or are forthcoming in *Boston Review, The Threepenny Review, Thrush, The Minnesota Review, Lavender, The Journal of Compressed Creative Arts, Fairy Tale Review, Say It Loud: Poems About James Brown* (Whirlwind Press), *Introduction to Poetry* (Kendall Hunt), and other journals and anthologies. She is a contributing editor at *The Writing Disorder*.

ABOUT INDOLENT BOOKS

Indolent Books is a small independent press founded in 2015 and operating in Brooklyn. Indolent was founded as a home for poets of a certain age who have done the creative work but for whatever reason (family, career, self-effacement, etc.) have not published a first collection. But we are not dogmatic about that mission: Ultimately, we publish books we like and care about, short or long, poetry or prose. We are queer owned, queer staffed, and maintain a commitment to diversity among our authors, artists, designers, developers, and other team members.

www.ingramcontent.com/pod-product-compliance
Lightning Source LLC
Chambersburg PA
CBHW021453080526
44588CB00009B/835